You are perhaps intrigued why a book first published in May 1909 is being republished over a hundred years later. The reason is a simple one: the issues it deals with are as relevant today as they were then.

As Dr Reinhardt says:

"After some research Professors Metchnikoff *(Nobel Prize Laureate),* Massol *and* Duclaux *traced the cause of the general soundness of health and durability of the vital organs and the tissues generally to the [Bulgarian] national habit of using a special form of sour-milk as a daily item in the diet. This curdled milk is prepared with a ferment known as Maya and the product is called* Yoghourt.."

This insightful book teaches you to protect your body from the multitude of toxins you almost certainly consume every day in one form or another.

Indeed, due to the way food is produced and processed today, this book's message is even more relevant now than it was a century ago.

I hope the knowledge contained in this short read will lead you and your family, friends and colleagues to a much healthier lifestyle. Once you've finished with the book, pass it onto a friend and they will be indebted to you forever; you'll certainly have extended someone's life by your kind actions.

Enjoy the benefits and joys of making your own homemade yogurt.

A mountain of thanks to Delia's Smith *(Delia's How To Cook: Book One)* and Doris Grant *(Your Daily Food: Recipe for Survival)* whose work laid the path to this wonderful book.

120YEARSOFLIFE.COM

First published 1909 by
The London Publicity Company Ltd
This edition
©2015 published by 120yearsoflife.com

ISBN 978-0-9566476-0-3

Printed in the China

120 YEARS OF LIFE

AND · HOW · TO · ATTAIN · THEM

· ·BY·CHARLES·REINHARDT·M·D·

A treatise upon the use of Lactic Ferments for
the prevention and cure of disease and the
prolongation of life.

PRICE ONE SHILLING.

THE LONDON PUBLICITY COMPANY, LIMITED,
379, STRAND, LONDON, W.C.

PREFACE.

The first part of this little treatise consists of a reprint of four articles which appeared in the "General Practitioner," the official organ of the General Medical Practitioners' Association, in January and February, 1909, under the headline "Elixir Vitae Nova."

The subject is one which has attracted attention for some time. Under the title "A New Elixir of Life," The British Medical Journal published a considerable amount of correspondence and some leading articles during 1908, and even the daily newspapers have made occasional references to the wonders of the Metchnikoff Sour-Milk treatment.

The time, therefore, seems ripe for the publication of a little handbook containing directions and precautions to be observed in the preparation of the sour milk.

In Southern Europe many of the peasants

live on little else beyond sour milk and bread, and they prepare the former without the advantage of any scientific knowledge of the processes involved. Such knowledge, however, cannot be out of place for those who would employ the Bulgarian methods to the fullest advantage, and it is with the object of offering the requisite information that this little book has been compiled.

CHARLES REINHARDT.

40, South Eaton Place,
       Eaton Square, S.W.
           May, 1909.

120 YEARS OF LIFE.

By Charles Reinhardt, M.D.

No method of medical treatment has aroused such widespread interest amongst the medical profession during recent years as that depending upon the administration of lactic ferments and lactic acid-producing bacilli.

The desire to experience length of life is a natural one, shared by all raced of mankind, and in a sense, at least, by the sub-human animals, who give lively evidence of the instinct of self-preservation. Amongst civilized humanity, however, the desire to live long is happily qualified by the wish to live well and to preserve good health. Every man and woman who was reached middle age, or even full maturity, knows that the fear of old age, with its enfeebled powers and increased liability to infirmity and suffering, is likely to develop from an unpleasant anticipation into an unhappy reality, and unless acute disease or accident prematurely end a life, senility supervenes, and the second childhood is entered "Sans teeth, sans eyes, sans taste, sans everything," as Shakespeare has it.

And after the second childhood comes inevitable death!

The old theories as to the cause of old age must be greatly modified in the light of the recent researches of Professor Metchnikoff, whose opinions on the subject have been so widely circulated and so unanimously accepted.

Professor Metchnikoff, the world-renowned pathologist of the Pasteur Institute, and Professor Duclaux, who was the director of the same institution, noticed when visiting Bulgaria, which has for many years been known as a country where human longevity is common, that not only did the inhabitants attain a remarkable age, but that the qualities of your were preserved almost till the end. Thus centenarians, of which amongst a population of less than three millions there are considerable more than three thousand, were found with unimpaired faculties performing duties which in this country would be considered too exacting for a man of seventy; moreover, in appearance and in demeanour, as well as in general health, these aged young men and women displayed a vigour and alertness of which persons of any age might well be proud. Upon enquiry Professor Metchnikoff made the astounding discovery that deaths at the age of a hundred and ten, fifteen, or even twenty years were by no means uncommon, though the conditions of life and the comparative poverty of the people suggested no explanation of their longevity.

After some research Professors Metchnikoff and Duclaux traced the cause of the general soundness of health and durability of the vital organs and the tissues generally to the national habit of using a special form of sour milk as a daily item in the dietary. This curdled milk is prepared with a ferment know as "Maya," and the product is called "Yoghourt," and amongst the Bulgarian peasants it may be said to form a staple article of food. It has often been observed in places nearer home than Bulgaria – for instance, in Scotland, Ireland, and Brittany – that the habit of drink-

ing buttermilk or soured milk seemed not only
to be a wholesome custom, but even one con-
ducive to length of life, but the sour milk of the
South European States differs from ordinary
whey in that it is prepared, not with rennet or
by churning, but by means of a living culture
of lactic-acid-forming bacilli, which survive
the passage through the human stomach and
become acclimatized in the intestinal tract, to
the comparative exclusion of putrefactive and
pathogenic organisms.

What is Old Age ?

The lines of enquiry suggested to Professor
Metchnikoff by his observations upon the
Bulgarian peasantry, finally led him to express
opinions of quite a revolutionary character on
the subject of age and senility. These conditions
are not to be considered, he said, as altogether
due to calcification of the arteries, hardening
of the nerve tissues, or a mere wearing out of
the organism, but they are rather to be regarded
as the effects of a chronic disease due to the
absorption from the intestines of toxins or
poisons produced by putrefactive processes

therein. The possession of a capacious colon or large intestine may be a convenience to civilized man, but it has its disadvantages, and it is probable that the morbid processes which go on within it not only shorten life but account for much misery and suffering and definite disease. In support of his theory Professor Metchnikoff points out that those creatures which either have no colon, or only a rudimentary organ fulfilling its purposes, are with one or two exceptions long lived, for instance parrots, crows, eagles and other birds live to an immense age, some of them perhaps for two hundred and fifty years, and the same may be said of tortoises, crocodiles and other creatures, which are either not provided with a large intestine, or are found upon investigation not to harbor in large quantities putrefactive micro-organisms in their alimentary canals.

Under ordinary circumstances the human bowel contains vast numbers of germs, which set up putrefactive processes, and give rise to the formation of ptomaines and other toxins, which, being absorbed into the blood, poison the tissues, finally leading to atrophy and degeneration and consequent inefficiency.

If this view of senility be accepted, the problem of the preservation of youth and the postponement of old age resolves itself into that of procuring a condition of comparative asepsis of the bowel. In other words, if the putrefactive and disease-producing germs which swarm in the intestine can be replaced by harmless bacilli which will crowd out and inhibit the growth of pathogenic or disease-producing organisms, the net result will be that the process of auto-intoxication of blood-poisoning by the absorption of the products of putrefaction will be prevented, and that the disease of old age will be warded off, or its advance retarded. But this is not all, for the very conditions which preserve the attributes of youth also protect the body from disease, and in cases where disease has already effected an invasion the introduction of a beneficent bacillus may compel the unwelcome intruder to evacuate the position.

A NATURAL METHOD.

The deliberate employment of microbes which confer a benefit upon their human host is, perhaps, a modern method without being a new one ; for though not consciously used, beneficent microbes have undoubtedly been pressed into service from the earliest ages.

As a single illustration of this fact, the use of buttermilk and soured milk by the inhabitants of Southern Europe, and elsewhere, forms, perhaps, the most striking case, though the same principle underlies the old tradition that certain mild ailments confer protection from other more serious, and it is upon the observation of phenomena of this kind by Jenner that the method of protection from small-pox by vaccination was founded. The difference between the hypotheses in the past and those of to-day depends solely upon the comparatively recent birth of the science of bacteriology, which as shown us that the natural methods by which disease is resisted and normal health preserved involve process-es which transform our bodies into countless battlefields in which invasions, sieges, routs, and massacres are common occurrences. These phenomena, indeed, amply justify the expression, "The romance of medicine," which has recently been applied to minutely accurate, but not the less marvelous, accounts of certain proceedings connected with metabolism, infection, inflammation, resolution, and various pathological and physiological activities.

We owe to Professor Metchnikoff the valuable discovery that the advantages enjoyed in Bulgaria, Servia, Roumania, and the adjacent countries by the peasants who regularly take their sour milk as a part of their food might be experienced elsewhere by anyone willing to take the necessary amount of trouble in preparing the "Yoghourt." These advantages are numerous and unmistakable, for in most cases the regular use of the lactic ferment is soon followed by increased comfort, and a freedom from digestive derangement, which in themselves are an ample compensation for the attention, care, and vigilance requisite for the efficient manufacture of the properly inoculated milk; to say nothing for the moment of the successful treatment of definitely morbid conditions, and the prolongation of life which the regular employment of cultures of lactic-acid-producing bacilli is believed to lead to.

How to Prepare the Sour Milk.

Before further discussing the therapeutical effects of the lactic ferments, it will be well to describe the mode of preparation to be employed. The process is simple enough if the directions and precautions are observed with scrupulous care. The requisites are a supply of pure fresh milk, free from chemical preservatives, such as boracic acid or formaldehyde. A saucepan with a lid, three or four common glass tumblers, or an earthenware jar, a box of ordinary children's nightlights, and an ordinary milk thermometer. These requirements can be readily furnished in any home, but if it is preferred a special appliance made in tin, aluminium, or copper can be bought for a few shillings to take the place of the kitchen pans. These appliances for the preparation of sour milk are generally made to accommodate three glass or porcelain tumblers, or one large jar, and the receptacle is raised upon a deep rim to accommodate the nightlight. The process, however, is the same, and the results identical, whether a specially designed contrivance is employed or the domestic utensils of the kitchen are pressed into the service provided always that the most punctilious cleanliness is observed. Under ordinary circumstances it is well not to employ kitchen utensils which are used for other purposes.

Let us assume for the moment, however, that no special appliances are available. The tumblers are filled with milk and placed in the saucepan, which is nearly filled with water, and the lid is applied. The milk is then gently brought to boiling point and maintained at that temperature for at least half an hour, or even an hour. This sterilizes the milk, killing any harmful microbes which it may have contained – for though it was stipulated that the milk should be fresh and pure, these conditions can seldom be guaranteed under the existing state of things, where the housing and milking of cows and the transportation, storage, and local distribution of milk are concerned. After having been well boiled, the milk is allowed to cool to body heat, that is to say, about 98 degrees F. This must be ascertained by means of a thermometer, as a few degrees of excessive heat will have an injurious effect upon the process of incubation. A small quantity of a culture of Bulgarian lactic-acid-forming bacilli is now added to each tumbler of milk, or if this is not the first day of preparation, a generous spoonful of the sour milk of the previous day will suffice to inoculate each tumbler of milk. The lid of the saucepan is then replaced, and a nightlight is lighted and set under the saucepan, which may be raised upon two bricks, or upon a small iron stand, which can be purchased at an ironmonger's shop for a few pence. The light should be from one to two inches below the bottom of the pan. The effect of the heat from the nightlight is to keep the temperature of the milk and of the water surrounding the tumblers at about 98 degrees in our climate, but in tropical climates, or in very hot weather, the artificial heat of the nightlight may be dispensed with. The temperature should be maintained at blood heat for ten hours, during which time the bacilli in the culture, or in the small portion of the previous day's sour milk, will have multiplied in the inoculated milk, which will have curdled and become semi-solid. The process should them be arrested by the withdrawal of the heat, and in cold weather it will suffice to place the saucepan, still covered, in a cool place, or if the weather is mild it may be allowed to stand upon ice for a further period of twelve hours, when it will be ready for consumption.

Mode of Consumption.

About a tumblerful should be taken twice of three times daily as a part of each meal, and it is an advantage both as to flavor and efficacy if a liberal amount of sugar be added, as the lactic acid is produced more generously when an ample amount of saccharine matter is present.

The first culture must be purchased from a reliable laboratory, but after one lot of sour milk has been prepared from such a culture, it will suffice, if pure milk be used, if the second day's milk be inoculated by the admixture of a spoonful of that of the first day, and so on ; always assuming that such care and cleanliness are exercised as will prevent the milk being contaminated by extraneous germs, which might alter the product, and thus prevent the development of the true lactic-acid-forming bacilli.

Extreme Cleanliness

One cannot be too careful in cleaning the utensils used. For instance, the tumblers should be washed in hot water which has reached boiling point, and been allowed to cool sufficiently, they should then be set to drain, and not wiped out with a cloth, which might introduce pathogenic organisms; the thermometer, spoons, and in fact all the appliances with which the milk comes in contact, should be treated with the same scrupulous regard to cleanliness.

The finished product should contain two per cent. of lactic acid, and should produce a definitely acid reaction if tested with blue litmus paper. It will not only contain this percentage of the actual acid, but it will be highly charged with active living Bulgarian bacilli which, though entirely harmless to the human body, are destructive to the germs which produce putrefaction, the fact being that the lactic-acid-forming bacilli are robust and resistant, and survive the pathogenic organisms which may find their way into the alimentary canal.

At the same time these beneficent germs act upon the sugary and starchy foods in such a manner as to produce further supplies of lactic acid in the lower alimentary canal, the contents of which are rendered acid in reaction, and comparatively aseptic in character. After a while the lactic bacilli become acclimatized, and then, even if the habit of taking the sour milk be discontinued, they will persist in the bowel for some days of weeks.

It has been estimated that the regular administration of the sour milk for a week will lead to the acclimatization of the beneficent bacilli in the intestines, and by this time, even if not from the time of the first doses, benefit should be noticed in all cases in which there has been suffering due to intestinal fermentation or putrefaction. And, indeed, as few persons are exempt from such processes, there are few who do not find benefit from the regular use of sour milk produced by Professor Metchnikoff's modification of the Bulgarian method.

ADDITIONAL PRECAUTIONS.

It has been pointed out that care must be taken to secure pure milk, to sterilize it, and to exercise strict cleanliness in the process of preparation. It should be added that it is of the utmost importance that a culture of the true Bulgarian bacilli should be secured at the outset. For it is to be remembered that there are over a hundred known species of lactic-acid-producing bacilli, and that the efficacy of the treatment depends upon the fact that the true Bulgarian bacilli are more active and more resistant than the other varieties. If sour milk produced by bacilli of feeble resisting power is taken, the beneficial results will be modified, and disappointment will be the result, whereas if contaminated cultures are used the net result may be positively harmful.

It is possible to buy tablets containing the Bulgarian bacilli, but I have obtained by far the most satisfactory results from liquid cultures, and it is, of course, more easy to secure the ingestion of a large number of the beneficent bacilli by incubating the germs in the milk as already described than by swallowing small tablets in the hope that the process of incubation may be carried on within the body. The one advantage of taking the tablets is the convenience of the process, and in cases where preparations of milk are considered unpalatable, or cannot be tolerated, the dry tablets may be tried. It is well that the treatment in all cases of ill-health should be pursued under medical supervision, and it is desirable that the physician should make frequent tests, so as to find out if the lactic-acid-producing bacilli are actually surviving the journey through the alimentary tract, and at least it should be ascertained whether or not the acid reaction to litmus paper is constant.

THERAPEUTICAL CONSIDERATIONS

It has long been recognized that lactic acid has valuable medicinal properties, though until recent times it has been considered impracticable to make good use of its therapeutic powers, though it has been administered as a digestive adjuvant in cases of dyspepsia, and it has even been employed in cases of diabetes. It is one thing, however, to give medicinal doses of dilute lactic acid, and another to administer a living culture of lactic-acid-producing bacilli, as in the former case the effect of the medicament is limited to the individual doses, which seldom reach the bowel unchanged, whereas in the latter the beneficent bacilli become acclimatized in the bowel and actually produce the lactic acid on the spot where it is capable of exerting its beneficial influence. Moreover, the presence of the acid renders the contents of the bowel a less congenial medium for the growth of pathogenic organisms, whilst the lactic acid bacilli actually destroy them ; the net result being a most healthful condition of bowel cleanliness which no other known medicinal agent can bring about.

Auto-Intoxication.

To arrive at an estimation of the therapeutic value of the lactic ferments it is necessary to inquire as to the ill-effects of the intestinal putrefaction which they are capable of diminishing or preventing. It is obvious that if decomposition is going on in the intestine, and of poisonous substances are being produced therein, there must be a danger of auto-intoxication or self-poisoning, since there is constant absorption going on from the intestines to the circulatory system. We know, in fact, that such auto-intoxication is almost constantly proceeding in all excepting those in normal health, and some suspect that the large number of diseases already believed to be directly due to such morbid processes will be greatly increased as our knowledge of the subject grows. It as already been suggested that old age is a chronic disease due, at least in part, to this cause, and it has long been recognized that minor ills such as headaches, migraine, and lassitude, are provoked by poisons absorbed from the digestive tract ; but in between senility and comparatively transient and trivial disorders are a large number of more or less serious conditions which may be traced to similar causes. Perhaps the most common, and the most amenable to the lactic treatment, is intestinal atony due to putrefaction. The symptoms include pain, distention, loss of appetite, and in some instances diarrhea. The disorder may be acute or chronic, and in either case may lead to appendicitis, colitis, or enteritis. Medicines may have been tried without success, or, indeed, they may have resulted in an increase of the disorder, and even the most carefully planned diet may have failed to give any relief to the sufferer, but the employment of sour milk prepared with the Bulgarian lactic-acid-producing culture will quickly cleanse the bowel, and, by removing the cause of the discomfort, abolish it. In these cases the first effect of the treatment is a sense of comfort and well-being, which is most encouraging alike to physician and patient. Discouragement, however, should not be felt if this immediate benefit is not experienced, for in come cases the beneficent bacilli do not at once colonise in the intestine, or are themselves overpowered by the antagonistic forces at work therein, and then for some time there may be no improvement, or, perhaps, even some temporary exacerbation of the symptoms may be produced.

POSSIBLE CAUSES OF FAILURE

It should not be overlooked, however, that such failure may be due to some omission or defect in the preparation or mode of administration of the ferment. It is assumed that a reliable culture has been obtained at the outset, and that care has been exercised to prevent contamination or deterioration, but in addition to this, the physician should make regular periodical examinations of the urine and faeces to ascertain in the first case if there is an excessive discharge of ethereal sulphates, which indicate auto-intoxication, and in the second, to see whether an acid reaction to litmus paper has been produced, and if, on the contrary, there are numerous organisms present. Normal human faeces, in the absence of putrefactive decomposition, are heavier than, and should sink in water; they should also be comparatively inodorous. It occasionally happens that an inefficient sour milk is taken patiently for a long period without benefit, simply for want of a thorough and systematic supervision. If the treatment is worth undertaking, and of this there can be no doubt, it is worth doing well.

Definate Disease.

In persons suffering from serious diseases due to structural changes a cure may be an impossibility, and yet benefit and alleviation may be achieved. Thus lactic ferments have been advantageously employed in cases of cancer of the stomach, Bright's disease, rheumatoid arthritis, and gout.

They have also been used with marked success in such functional disorders as constipation, anaemia, neurasthenia, and chronic ill-health without apparent cause.

The Bulgarian lactic-acid-producing bacillus is believed to be capable of destroying the typhoid bacillus, and, therefore, sour milk has been given in cases of enteric fever, and it has been tried with considerable promise of success in the case of typhoid carriers, who continue to harbor and periodically eject and disseminate the typhoid bacillus after apparent recovery from enteric fever. The problem of the typhoid carrier is a serious one, and if the lactic acid bacillus can cope with that of Eberth, its early solution will be within the bounds of possibility.

SOUR MILK AS A FOOD

It must not be forgotten that Bulgarian sour milk is an excellent food, having the nutrient qualities of milk without presenting the difficulties which that aliment sometimes offers to the digestion. Moreover, when well prepared, and served with sugar, sour-milk is a dish which most patients enjoy, and the appetite for it grows by what it feeds upon, so that occasionally a patient who dislikes it at the first trial will become extremely fond of it after a while. There is the advantage to be remembered that its use may be temporarily suspended without the loss of the therapeutic effects, for the bacilli once acclimatized in the bowel will continue to multiply and exert their beneficent influence for several weeks after the ingestion of fresh supplies has ceased.

It may be well to recapitulate the directions for preparing and administering the Bulgarian sour milk as follows : —

Obtain pure milk—the presence of any chemical preservative, such as boracic acid or formaline, will precent the fermentative process—place the milk in one or more common glass tumblers or an earthenware jar, and stand these in a saucepan half filled with tepid water, cover with the lid, and place on the kitchen range or a gas stove, so as to bring the water to boiling point. Boil for a least half an hour, and set aside to cool (a full hour's boiling is by some considered desirable). When the milk has cooled to about 98 degrees Fahrenheit, add the culture of ferment, either obtained for the purpose or preserved from the former day's sour milk, and keep the milk at the same temperature for ten hours. This can be done by placing the saucepan, in which the milk was boiled, with the milk still contained in the tumblers, over a ten hours night light, and leaving it till the light has burnt out, when the saucepan and contents should be set aside in a cool place for about twelve hours.

The sour milk will now be thick and cream-like, though the consistency varies according to the length of time that it is kept; the medicinal qualities, however, are not disturbed by the alteration in thickness, which is due to a partial reabsorption of the clot.

If preferred a special apparatus can be procured, and this is, generally speaking, a more satisfactory course than that of using ordinary kitchen utensils. In this case the milk may be boiled in the jar placed in a covered saucepan half full of water, the jar afterwards being placed in the special sour milk apparatus.

Observe strict cleanliness throughout the whole process. The culture or ferment once obtained would continue to produce the sour milk indefinitely, as a few teaspoonfuls from to-day's sour milk will act as the ferment for that to be prepared for to-morrow's use. It is well, however, to obtain a fresh culture from time to time, since it is difficult to avoid occasional contamination with undesirable germs.

Test the sour milk occasionally with blue litmus paper, which should turn red promptly and decidedly directly it comes in contact with the milk.

Take about a tumbler full of sour-milk two or three times daily well sweetened with sugar. The sour milk renders the sugar easy of digestion, and the sugar promotes the production of the lactic acid; moreover, the sweetened preparation is very pleasant to the palate. It may be taken with or independently of the ordinary meals.

Where pure fresh mill cannot be obtained, condensed milk may be employed with satisfactory results.

The cases in which Bulgarian sour milk may be used with advantage are numerous, and may be outlined as follows :-

(1) Constipation, intestinal atony, enteritis, threatened appendicitis, diarrhea, flatulence, and all conditions due to local putrefactive processes.

(2) Dyspepsia, hepatic troubles, gallstone, migraine, and all secondary effects of intestinal sepsis.

(3) Typhoid fever and its sequelae, diabetes, boils, pimples, nettle rash, and eczema.

(4) Blood disorders, including gout, rheumatoid arthritis, arterio-sclerosis, etc.

(5) Lastly, it must be remembered that sour milk is an excellent food both for children and adults ; indeed, its regular use sometimes appears to diminish the appetite, in that it replaces other aliments. The Bulgarian peasants live on little else beyond bread and sour milk. The continued use of sour milk is believed, with good reason, to preserve youth, and to retard the onset of all the symptoms associated with old age. Metchnikoff's milk is largely used in Sanatoria for Consumptives with very beneficial results, leading to an increase in weight, and a general improvement in health.

There are few persons who do not find marked benefit follow a course of Bulgarian sour milk, and in no case can it prove harmful. It should be continued for at least three months if a satisfactory trial is to be made, and there is no reason against its permanent continuance.

It has been suggested that the habit of making sub-cultures, that is of preparing one day's sour-milk by the addition of a portion of that of the day before, has the possible disadvantage that the product may become accidentally contaminated, and that after a while an unsatisfactory and an impure sour-milk may be produced, and that it is possible, where contaminated milk has been used at the outset, heat resisting spores might escape sterilization in the preliminary boiling process, and that they might develop activity during the process of incubation. The best answer to this seems to be that in Bulgaria, Southern Russia, Turkey, and other places sour milk has been prepared daily for ages without any of the precautions that we now recommend, and with eminently satisfactory practical results ; moreover, even if the milk does contain pathogenic organisms the presence of the lactic-acid-producing bacilli in overwhelming numbers, and the resulting acidity of the milk, would render the latter an uncongenial medium for their growth; nevertheless, as already pointed out, it is as well to obtain fresh culture from a reliable source about once in every three weeks, or immediately in the event of the sour-milk becoming in any way unpleasant or unpalatable, since the milk supply in this country, unfortunately, is seldom above suspicion.

PREPARATORY MEDICATION

It has been made perfectly clear that the presence of any chemical antiseptic in the milk used for the preparation of Bulgarian Sour Milk will prove fatal to the fermentative process, and the same principle applies in cases in which persons who are taking the Sour Milk, at the same time take medicines which may contain chemical substances capable of arresting the process of bacterial reproduction. There is no objection, however, to a preliminary course of medicinal treatment, with the object of preparing the alimentary system for the work which is to be carried on by the Lactic-Acid-producing bacilli. Under ordinary circumstances amongst persons living sedentary lives in cities the number of germs infesting the bowel is astonishingly great, amounting to as many as twelve millions per gramme of contents. It is clear, therefore, that when the Lactic Acid treatment is first commenced the beneficent germs have a great task to overcome before they can themselves become predominant in number : and therefore, if a method can be devised by which the task can be rendered more easy, the patient will derive corresponding benefit.

With this object in view, it occurred to me that it might be advantageous before commencing the ferment treatment to take steps to weaken the enemy or to drive it out altogether by means of Cyllin, which I had previously employed with good results amongst patients suffering from tuberculosis with enteric symptoms.

Cyllin is a disinfectant twenty times as strong as pure carbolic acid, and yet, given in medicinal doses, non-poisonous ; it has proved very successful in the treatment of various diseases such as infantile diarrhea, dysentery, consumption of the bowels, as well as various tropical disorders of a dysenteric type.

Cyllin in administered in the form of palatinoids for adults, and "Cyllin Syrup" for children. The palatinoids have the advantage of not dissolving until they reach the intestines, being prepared by Jeyes' Sanitary

Compounds Company in two qualities, one suitable for stomachic medication being enclosed in comparatively thin and solvent envelopes, whilst the other, which should be used for the purpose now under consideration, are covered by capsules which resist the digestive secretion, whilst dissolving readily in the bowel.

I tried this preliminary Cyllin treatment with satisfactory results in several cases in which there appeared to be an unusual amount of intestinal putrefaction, and provided that it is regarded as a preliminary method, and that the Sour Milk treatment is not commenced until a sufficient time has elapsed to ensure the complete elimination of the antiseptic, I regard it as a valuable auxiliary.

Lactic Acid Preparations

I have purposely dwelt at some length and even with reiteration, upon the method of preparing the sour-milt at home, for there are advantages in adopting this procedure, one of which is economy, since the sour-milk costs little more than the price of the fresh milk used, or four pence a quart. The finished product, moreover, is more nourishing, more digestible, and more solid than fresh milk, and thus on the ground of cheapness alone it may be recommended as an article of diet.

There are many, however, who will not wish to encounter the trouble involved, or who may be so placed that it would be impracticable to perform the process. For such cases there are a number of preparations available which contain the lactic-acid-producing bacilli. Several diaries supply the-sour milk ready made, but caution must be observed in accepting from an ordinary dairyman a preparation requiring such delicate handling, and such an amount of technical bacteriological information as sour-milk, especially in view of the fact that the milk supply of London is found to be more or less contaminated in about ninety-two per cent. of all samples obtainable.

The London Pure Milk Association.

It is a pleasure, therefore, to note the establishment of the London Pure Milk Association, which supplies pure and reliable milk in

sealed and dated bottles only, thus supersed-
ing the old insanitary metal milk can, and the
dirty and dangerous habit of mixing milk in-
discriminately, and purveying it in open churns
or containers, which nothing short of a sanitary miracle can keep clean. This association
has obtained the sole British concession from
the "Societe Le Ferment," of Paris, which is the
sole purveyor of sour-milk to Professor Metchnikoff himself, and it is now prepared to sell
sour-milk in London under the name "Lacto-
bacilline Milk" in sealed opal bottles at 9d. and
1s. 3d. each.

I am glad to take the opportunity of
recommending all who realize the dangers
of an impure milk supply, and this should
include all prudent housekeepers, to obtain
their milk from the Pure Milk Association,
which has depots in various parts of London.

One of the special products of this
Company is Homogenised Milk, which
consists of milk forced under great pressure
through a small jet, against a smooth piece
of agate, the result being that the fat globules
are broken up into such small particles as to

render it practically impossible to abstract the cream by any process whatever ; the fluid becoming homogeneous, and in fact a much more perfect emulsion than natural milk, and, as a consequence, more readily digestible. Homogenised milk makes excellent sour milk of the consistency of thick cream, and if it be previously sterilized, the preliminary process of boiling is rendered unnecessary.

Another dairy which may be strongly recommended is that of Messrs. Clay, Paget and Company, Ltd., which has long been favourably know to the medical profession for the excellence of its preparations of humanized, peptonised, sterilized and diabetic sugar-free milk, and which has now taken up the preparation of soured milk.

Those who use Bulgarian sour-milk cultures on a large scale may obtain them from Messrs. Oppenheimer, of Queen Victoria Street. This firm has devoted considerable attention to this question, and the cultures supplied by it are eminently reliable. They are packed in boxes containing twelve tubes, under the name "Lactigen," the price per box being 4s.

6d. ; each tube being sufficient for one pint of milk. Messrs. Oppenheimer supply several of the dairy companies.

Those who require a single culture at a time, for the purpose of making the sour milk at home, can obtain it from the Veronelle Company already referred to. This Company has also prepared the Bulgarian bacilli in a form which is sure to become extremely popular alike on account of its efficacy and it convenience. This is the Veronelle Romaya cream, which consists practically of solid sour milk of the consistency of an ordinary cream cheese or "petit Suisse." It may be eaten with sugar by children or with pepper and salt by adults who may prefer it so ; or it may be mixed with cold milk and used in a semi-liquid form. It has the advantage of convenience of transit and of its keeping qualities. It may be used to replace a culture in the preparation of further supplies of sour milk, and its invariable success in this respect proves that it contains the living lactic acid bacilli in unimpaired condition. The Veronelle Romaya cream is sold in boxes at 1s. 2d. It is prepared at a country farm dairy under the supervision of a milk bacteriologist of long experience, but it may be obtained from the London order office of the Veronelle Company, 55, Sidmouth Street, W.C.

LACTIC TABLETS

Several firms supply tablets containing the Bulgarian bacilli. In some cases the product is not reliable, since it is difficult to preserve a pure and active culture in the form of a dry tablet. I have, however, obtained good results from those made by Messrs. Allen and Hanbury, under the name "Sauerin," and those prepared by Messrs. Cox, of Brighton.

Some of the tablets which I have examined have proved to be practically inert, which may have been due to their having been packed for some time. Tablets of reliable quality, such as those mentioned, may be used either to prepare sour milk or for direct internal administration. I always prefer, however, to administer the actual sour milk, excepting in cases where milk in any form is objected to, when the tablets may be tried.

Another convenient form in which the

Bulgarian bacilli may be obtained is that of the "Oxygal" granules which are prepared by a process devised by Doctor Stassano, a member of the Society of Medicine of Paris. These may be strongly recommended.

GENERAL CONSIDERATIONS.

Having dealt with the preparation and use of sour-milk and the role played by the lactic acid and the lactic bacilli in the prevention of intestinal putrefaction, we may devote a few words to a consideration of the subject of old age generally, and also of morbid conditions now known to be dependent upon intestinal sepsis.

Sir James Crichton Browne says that "every man is entitled to his century, and every women to a century and a little more, for women live longer than men. Every child should be brought up impressed with the obligation of living to a hundred, and should be taught how to avoid the irregularities that tend to frustrate that laudable ambition"; whilst Metchnikoff tells us that the inmost convictions of man assure him that the present duration of life is too short, and that in his opinion a science of the prolongation of life should be built up. On the other hand, we have Professor Osler, who contends that the best work of life is performed before the age of 40, and that it would be advantageous to mankind were the habit of retiring from active work at an age limit of sixty years generally insisted upon.

I am inclined to agree with Metchnikoff, and to disagree completely with Osler, who seems to have overlooked the fact that many of the highest human achievements have been made by men well over his age limit; and that in many spheres of activity improved capacity is constantly evolved, until a much later stage of maturity.

In China, a man of forty is not looked upon as old. In the words of Confucius, "Until a man is thirty, he is like the ivy or the vine, with no inherent strength, at forty he is a bare tree, at fifty he puts forth leaves, at seventy fruit."

Palmerston, Beaconsfield, and Gladstone were young statesmen at seventy, Gladstone was Prime Minister when an octogenarian. Voltaire was a power in France when well over eighty, Michael Angelo was designing pictures for the churches in Rome at a similar age, and to-day we have General Booth of the

Salvation Army planning world-wide lecturing tours after having celebrated his eightieth birthday, and Frith, the artist, is well on in the nineties. In the "Daily Telegraph" of Easter Monday of this year (April 12th, 1909) amongst the obituary notices appear the names of four centenarians who died during the previous week, and one of these was an old lady of 110 years, who recently lost her husband, who had himself reached the age of 108. In the daily papers of April 17th, 1909, it is recorded that the Rector of Weston-under-Pengard, Herefordshire, The Rev. E. B. Hawkshaw, is performing his duties at the age of 94, and that another venerable cleric, the Rev. R. L. Alnutt, took part in the church service on Easter Sunday at the age of 92. And yet in proportion to the population, we have only one centenarian in this country to one hundred and eighty-seven in Bulgaria where sour-milk has been the national diet for ages.

A SIMPLE THEORY

The difference between the body of a child and that of an aged person is largely dependent upon the fact that the arteries in the infant are soft and elastic, whereas every day of life, involving as it does the frequently repeated circulation of the blood throughout the whole organism and the deposit of minute quantities of calcareous matter in the coats of the arteries, inevitably renders these blood carriers less resilient as time goes on. In very old persons they become rigid and brittle, and they can then no longer efficiently perform their functions. An old person is one whose arteries are hard and inelastic, as a consequence of which the nourishment of every part suffers. The brain and medulla not receiving the requisite flow of blood, formerly regulated by the elasticity of the arteries, become in turn sluggish and irresponsive; the heart fails, and there is a general wearing out of the tissues of the whole body. This process is progressive and inevitable, but Metchnikoff has shown us that it is greatly accelerated by the continual absorption of poisonous matters from the bowel; and it is a proper inference, that by preventing intestinal putrefaction, we delay the process of calcareous degeneration of the blood vessels, and thus preserve youth or retard the advance of senility.

Intestinal putrefaction and the consequent auto-intoxication, or self-poisoning, are responsible, as already indicated, for many evils besides senile decay, but particularly for three of which we have heard a great deal of late years, namely appendicitis, neurasthenia, and neuritis. It is not too much to say that steps which will put an end to putrefaction in the intestine will invariably secure immunity from the three prevalent diseases just mentioned.

To Prevent Intestinal Putrefaction.

It is not wise to rely solely upon the use of sour-milk, but rather to further assist nature by avoiding the causes of intestinal putrefaction. Practically all the modern authorities are agreed that this condition is the result of errors in diet, one of the commonest of which is the excessive consumption of meat. Dr. Humphry, in his standard work on old age written nearly thirty years ago, stated that he had ascertained that practically all centenarians had been small meat eaters. Dr. Herschell, in his work on lactic ferments, expresses the conviction that one of the chief causes of the great prevalence of intestinal putrefaction and auto-intoxication at the present day is the excessive use of animal food. Metchnikoff has given expression to similar views.

The inevitable conclusion to which we are forced is that the chief cause of physical suffering, disease, and premature old age is the fact that few persons take the diet best suited to their requirements. The average individual has little knowledge of the science of dietetics, and medical men have too often contented themselves with prescribing medicines, instead of regulating the food, both as to quantity and quality. Whilst on the other hand, extremists have advocated set rules which might apply in certain instances, though producing disastrous results in others.

The advances in physiological science, and in the chemistry of foods and of the human body, have placed in the hands of the expert an instrument of precision not formerly available. As a single instance the fact may be mentioned that by a chemical examination of the urine and by a quantitive analysis, showing the amount of ethereal sulphates, indol, and phenol present, it is possible to learn if intestinal putrefaction is taking place, and to what extent ; and the actual results of the treatment adopted can be estimated in a manner independent of the patient's own account of his feelings, symptoms, and personal experiences.

There is, indeed, no more important and useful field of work for the physician at the present time, that that of dietetics.

DIET VERSUS DRUGS

It is probable that more can be accomplished by careful and scientific regulation of the diet to individual needs, than by the use of all the contents of the Pharmacopoeia. But hard and fast rules will not apply to all cases. A "purin free" diet may be salvation to one sufferer, whilst another may derive benefit from a temporary employment of an almost exclusively carnivorous regimen on the "Salisbury plan." A patient incapable of digesting starch, may need a diet from which this food is eliminated ; and I have seen most gratifying results follow in cases of profound directive impairment when the diet of a Bulgarian peasant, consisting almost exclusively of sour milk and bread, was adopted for a while. Intestinal putrefaction is the chief cause of ill-health among civilized communities to-day, and the most successful remedy is a scientific dietary, including the use of lactic ferments.

Sir Hermann Weber's Rules

It goes without saying that everyone who is anxious to preserve good health and the attributes of youth, should obey all the known rules of hygiene, which, according to Sir Hermann Weber, include the following :—

Observe moderation in food and drink and all other physical pleasures. Breathe pure air at all times. Take regular daily exercise whatever the weather. Go to bed early and rise early. Take a daily bath and let the skin be well rubbed. Perform work regularly and cultivate a hopeful or optimistic disposition. Avoid alcohol and other stimulants and narcotic drugs, and finally make a resolute effort of will to preserve health and life. Metchnikoff accepts and adopts these rules with the very important addition that he recommends the regular consumption of sourmilk, containing the Bulgarian lactic-acid-producing bacilli, and, lest the uninformed should have misgivings, he concludes with words which I quote as follow: "the inexperienced reader may be surprised at our suggesting the introduction of large quantities of microbes, the popular idea being that microbes are necessarily noxious. That view, however, is altogether erroneous, for there are useful microbes, and among them the lactic organism takes a foremost place."

DIRECTIONS FOR PREPARING METCHNIKOFF MILK WITH THE VERONELLE APPARATUS.

Boil a pint or more of pure milk in the earthenware jar standing in a saucepan of water. Let the milk boil for at least half an hour.

When cooled to 98 deg. F., about the temperature of the human body, place the milk in the earthenware jar in the Veronelle incubator, surrounded by water of the same temperature Light an ordinary ten-hour child's night-light, and place under the apparatus. This maintains the temperature at about 98 to 110 degs. Add a tablespoonful of the culture to each half-pint of milk. After ten or twelve hours, when the light has burnt out, set the milk aside in a cool place for a similar period when it will be ready for use.

A tablespoonful of to-day's sour-milk added to the next day's milk acts as a ferment, so that one supply of the culture lasts for some time, but a fresh culture should be obtained at intervals to ensure a perfect product.

Do not add the culture till the milk is

cooled to about 100 degs., a higher temperature than 120 degs. will destroy its activity.

Always place the night-light in a saucer
of water before lighting and let it stand in it,
otherwise the wax will melt and the light will
burn out too soon.

Some persons suppose that the routine for
the preparation of sour milk is too trouble-
some to be undertaken lightly, but this is not
the case, for apart from the boiling of the milk,
which can be done by the cook in the kitchen,
the remainder of the process need not occupy
more than a couple of minutes. It is best done
at bedtime.

When made the sour milk will keep several
days, and it improves in flavor and consistency for about 36 hours.

A liberal supply of sugar should be served
with the milk. When habitually taking the
Bulgarian sour milk sugary and starchy foods
are digested with greater ease than ordinarily.

In some cases the best results are obtained
if an almost exclusively vegetarian regimen is
temporarily adopted.

As the amount of heat communicated to the contents of the incubator by a nightlight varies according to the temperature of the atmosphere and the quality of the nightlight, the Veronelle apparatus has been designed to admit of effective regulation of the temperature. Two stands are provided, one of wire and the second of perforated tin. Under ordinary circumstances, the incubator is placed on the tin stand and the whole apparatus is raised upon the wire stand.

In very cold weather the wire stand may be dispensed with, this brings the flame nearer the container and conserves the heat.

In warm weather the tin stand may be dispensed with, this leaves the flame less protected and allows the excess heat to escape.

The temperature should not be less than 90 or more than 110 degs.

The apparatus should be washed and dried after use.